Love the One You're With

Love
the One
You're
With

*Re-Energize the Passion
in Your Marriage*

Lee Ellis, LCSW

NEW YORK

LONDON • NASHVILLE • MELBOURNE • VANCOUVER

Love the One You're With

Re-Energize the Passion in Your Marriage

© 2020 Lee Ellis, LCSW

Published in New York, New York, by Morgan James Publishing in partnership with Difference Press. Morgan James is a trademark of Morgan James, LLC.
www.MorganJamesPublishing.com

ISBN 9781642794304 paperback
ISBN 9781642794311 eBook
Library of Congress Control Number: 2019900254

Cover Design by:
Chris Treccani
www.3dogcreative.net

Interior Design by:
Christopher Kirk
www.GFSstudio.com

Morgan James is a proud partner of Habitat for Humanity Peninsula and Greater Williamsburg. Partners in building since 2006.

Get involved today! Visit
MorganJamesPublishing.com/giving-back

To my husband, Ben, and my daughter, Hallie, for giving me a reason to find out what it takes to keep a family together. I love you both with all my heart.

Table of Contents

Introduction

*"When I was five years old, my mother always
told me that happiness was the key to life.
When I went to school, they asked me what I
wanted to be when I grew up. I wrote down
"happy." They told me I didn't understand the
assignment, and I told them they
didn't understand life."*
– John Lennon

I bet you had an idea of how you wanted your life to turn out when you were a kid. If you are like most people, you thought you would get married, have a house, a job, two kids, a dog or a cat, and you would live happily ever after.

Either you idealized your parents' marriage, or you didn't want to turn out like them. Either way, you dreamed that you would find the right person, get married, and it would be easy.

I fall into the category of idealizing my parents' marriage. I always dreamed that I would end up just like them as I watched them dance, while my dad kissed my mom and whispered, "I love you," in her ear. Imagine my surprise when my mom picked me up from a friend's house at the age of 14 and told me they had decided to separate. My dad never came back to the house and they got a divorce a year later. What do you think that experience taught me?

Now that you are married, you realize it's not as easy as you thought it would be when you were a kid. You're probably wondering if you should go ahead and get a divorce before you end up trapped, with kids and no way out. Maybe you think you married the wrong person because that spark just isn't there anymore. With the divorce rate in the United States being 40 to 50 percent and the rate for subsequent marriages even higher, it would be hard to not at least think of divorce as an option.

I bet you would give anything to go back to the way you felt about your partner at the beginning of the relationship, when conversation flowed easily, and passion was a given. Back to when their habits didn't annoy you and their words were almost always kind. What if you never get that back and things just continue to get worse? An unhappy marriage can make you feel like your entire life is miserable.

But what if you could be happy in your marriage again? What if you could actually have an even deeper connection than you ever imagined possible? Picture yourself ten years from now, having stayed in your marriage, and having a stronger relationship than ever. Picture yourself having a happy family, taking vacations together, and living life to the fullest.

The truth is that most marriages go through at least one rough period where divorce is a consideration. The good news is that, according to a study by Linda Waite, two out of three unhappily married adults who avoided divorce or separation ended up happily married five years later.

My desire for you is that you read this book and find out that you *can* turn your marriage around. I want you to put down this book and not only be inspired to stay in your marriage, but I want you to have a plan of action and the motivation to carry it out. I know your dream come true is to save this marriage and I want to help you do it.

I am going to give you a lot of information in

this book. You will start to understand why things in your marriage have gone wrong and why things you have tried haven't worked. You will see why so many marriages fail, and how you can beat the statistics. You will have all the information and help needed to be successful.

I know this can be scary. If your only two choices are to stay in an unhappy marriage or get a divorce, your near future looks grim. But I want you to hang in there and know that there is hope. With the information in this book, you can do what it takes to get the passion back in your marriage and in your life.

Chapter 1:

Where Did the Spark Go?

*"Experts on romance say for a happy marriage
there has to be more than a passionate love.
For a lasting union, they insist, there must be
a genuine liking for each other. Which, in my
book, is a good definition for friendship."*
– Marilyn Monroe

Tammy met Chad at a party during her senior year in college. She was immediately attracted to him, and he asked her out on a date. She was nervous at first, but they had so much in common that conversation was easy. They became inseparable in a very short amount of time, and when they weren't together, Tammy couldn't stop thinking about Chad. They emailed and texted even when they were supposed to be studying or working.

When Tammy talked about Chad, her face lit up, and she was sure this is what it means to fall in love. Chad felt the same way, and shortly after graduation, he proposed.

The wedding was perfect, but not as perfect as the honeymoon. They just couldn't get enough of each other. But a few months later, life seemed to be getting in the way of their relationship and passion. They were both working long hours, and their hours did not always coincide, so they didn't see each other as much as they did before they got married. When they did spend time together, they didn't have as much to talk about as they once did. They also didn't seem as passionate in the bedroom and their sex life suffered. Tammy started to worry. Had she married the wrong person? Had Chad already lost interest in her? What did she do wrong? Why didn't they seem to feel the same way about each other?

As time went on, Tammy noticed that Chad had some annoying habits. When she got home, she would become annoyed almost instantly if she noticed that he left his dirty dishes in the sink or hadn't made the bed when he was the last one to get up. They started bickering about the cleanliness of the house and keeping score of whose turn it was to do the laundry.

Falling in Love

When I ask my clients to tell me about how they first met their partners, their faces almost invariably light up. As they recall how they were feeling in the beginning, I can see the excitement and passion in their eyes. The mere question puts them in a sort of dreamy state. Falling in love is magical.

Think back to when you first fell in love with your husband or wife. Can you get into that dreamy sort of state too? In the beginning, connection is easy and the energy flowing between you is intense, joyful, and amazing. You feel like you just want to eat the other person up. You think about them non-stop, and you can't imagine that there will ever be a time when you feel differently about them. You are literally obsessed, and you never want the feeling to end.

In the beginning, the kindness between you makes you feel like you have finally met the person you were meant to be with for the rest of your life. You want to cook them dinner, give them a full body massage, and bring them coffee in the morning. You feel like you have finally met your soul mate.

What Happened to Us?

After a while, the feeling that your partner can "do no wrong" seems to fade. You start to notice things about them you didn't notice before. You are not as kind to each other, and doing nice things for them starts to feel more like a chore.

The effortless romantic passion you have for your partner fades over time as well. You no longer feel like you could spend the rest of your days gazing into their eyes. You no longer think about them all day when you are at work. The amount of time you spend texting back and forth diminishes more and more. It can start to feel like something has gone badly wrong. *Did I make a mistake by marrying this person?*

The "In Love" Chemicals

A story like this is very common. You fall in love and it's easy. You think you will always feel that way, and you get married because you never want to lose that feeling.

What you were never taught before you fell in love, is that the feeling of "in love" is actually caused by a flood of feel-good chemicals secreted by the body. Specifically, these chemicals include dopamine, adrenaline, and norepinephrine. The dopamine makes

you feel euphoric. The adrenaline and norepinephrine make you have those obsessive feelings that are
responsible for you thinking about the other person
non-stop and wanting to spend every moment with
them. They also increase your sex drive and attraction.
This falls into that category of "You were made that
way to make sure you procreate."

What do you think happens to those chemicals
over a period of time? They go back to normal levels.
So, because you don't have those same euphoric feelings anymore, and you are no longer obsessed and
preoccupied with thinking about the other person
and wanting to have sex all the time, you think something is wrong. You might even think you married the
wrong person.

The truth is that the passionate love you feel for
your partner at the beginning matures to a healthy,
stable companionship over time *if it is nurtured*. You
can make that happen by doing the things I recommend in this book, and you can have times where you
feel that spark again. You can have a deeper love than
you ever imagined possible, and even feel like you are
in love with life.

Chapter 2:

My Story

*"I have always believed, and I still believe,
that whatever good or bad fortune may come
our way we can always give it meaning and
transform it into something of value."*
– Hermann Hesse

I Understand What You're Going Through

When I was in junior high, I had a major crush on one of my brother's friends. He was four years older than me, so I knew I didn't have a chance with him, but we did become friends over the years. He used to pick me up when I needed a ride before I was old enough to drive. Looking back on it, he also had feelings for me, but in his mind, it wasn't appropriate given our age difference.

11

After high school, I moved away to go to college. My brother died in an accident when I was a senior, so I moved back to my home town after college to be close to my parents. I started spending a lot of time with my brother's friend and we were both still grieving from the loss. We went camping, cooked dinner, watched movies together, and basically did all the things a couple would do.

Eventually I signed up for a program to teach English in Mexico. Two days before I left, I was telling my brother's friend how awesome I thought he was and he kissed me. I thought about it a lot that night and the next day and decided it would be a terrible mistake to chance messing up our friendship by dating, especially since I was about to be in another country for five months. When I told him what I was thinking, he told me he would like to date me if I ever changed my mind.

The next day I was on a plane to Mexico. I couldn't stop thinking about the prospect of being with him and I even cried when I thought about it. I could come up with a million reasons why we would be a good match. When I got to Mexico I wrote him a letter telling him how I felt about him, including the fact that I never understood why people cried when they were happy before. But I was still scared to ruin our friendship, so

I sat on the letter for a couple of months. When I still felt the same way after thinking about it for a while, I sent him the letter. At that time, I swore to myself that if we took our friendship to another level, we would get married and stay together forever.

When the program was over, and I went back home, needless to say we were excited to see each other. We started dating and had a great time at first, but the spark that I expected was really never there. However, I had made a promise to myself that if I dated him I would stay with him for the rest of my life, so I lied to myself.

A few years later, we got married and looking back on it, I already knew something was wrong. I was able to convince myself that we had something that most couples didn't have though, since we had such a strong friendship.

Unhappiness started creeping in, and I pushed it down over and over. Eventually I couldn't ignore it anymore and sometimes I would go over to my mom's house when she wasn't there to curl up in a ball and cry. I felt so trapped, and I didn't want him to know.

My Experience with Traditional Therapy

As graduate school was nearing the end, our plan was to start having kids. I was panicked. I was so scared to get trapped in the marriage, but I was also terrified to leave. I decided to go to therapy to "fix" the marriage.

Therapy was a really good experience for me at first. I figured out why I felt so alone as a child and why I didn't feel deeply connected with anyone. My therapist said it was possible to fix the marriage, but he told a story about himself that changed my mind. He said he was married for several years, and they were at a couples' retreat when someone came around to check on them. He said all of the sudden it occurred to him that he already knew how to do the work to save his marriage, but he didn't want to do the work *with her.* When he told this story, it resonated so much with me that I immediately knew I didn't want to save my marriage either.

I still wasn't willing to give up though, so my husband and I started going to couple's counseling. It made us both extremely uncomfortable and things didn't get better. Then one day in a session, my husband had a lightbulb moment where he realized that spark had never been there for me. We both knew it was over at that moment.

Going through the divorce was absolutely grueling. My worst fear regarding that relationship had come true: I broke his heart and ruined our friendship.

I stayed in therapy for years after my divorce to work on myself. I wanted to heal as much as I could, so I could be in a healthy relationship and have a happy life. Therapy helped up until a point, but I reached a time where I was no longer receiving any benefits, so I stopped.

Becoming a Psychotherapist

Through this time, I was a new therapist myself. In my first job out of graduate school, I was working with children and families. I cringe when I think about how little I knew about how to help them back then.

That all changed when a researcher and PhD psychologist took me under her wing and trained me in a parenting intervention called *The Incredible Years*. I began leading parenting groups, and I watched everything change for these families.

There were many principles in *The Incredible Years*, but the principle that had the biggest impact on families was called "The Attention Principle." It stated that you get more of whatever behavior you focus your attention on. So, if you praise and reward the positive things your kids are doing, you will see more of that behavior. But on the flip side, if you focus on and talk about, yell, or criticize the negative behavior, you will also see more of it. At the time I didn't understand why this worked so well for parents, but now I do, and you will too by the end of this book.

A few years later, the same researcher trained me in a very well-known and widely used intervention called Cognitive Behavioral Therapy. The main idea behind this intervention is that your thoughts are directly related to the way you feel and the way you behave. Clients are asked to pay attention to their thoughts and change them to better feeling thoughts. This intervention worked if the clients were diligent about journaling and challenging their limiting beliefs, but most of them felt like it was too much work and they didn't follow through with the assignments. However, years later I figured out why this intervention can work if you stick with it.

Taking Therapy to Another Level

After a while, I started getting bored doing the same things over and over with clients, and I wasn't seeing the kind of results I would have liked. Maybe that is one reason that at the same time I was using these "evidence-based" interventions on my clients, I was seeking alternative techniques to help heal myself.

On some level, I knew my clients and I needed some kind of deeper healing.

Years later when I got married again, I felt like I was ready after being in therapy for years, and this time I married someone who had everything I wanted. We had the friendship and common interests, we were compatible in all the ways I thought were important, and we definitely had that "spark." But soon the fears crept in. What if I married the wrong person again? What if this marriage fails just like the last one and I have to get another divorce? What if it's just not possible for me to stay in a relationship?

Luckily, this time I knew I did want to save my marriage. Remember at the beginning of the book, I asked what it taught me when my seemingly happy parents got a divorce? Well, I discovered it taught me that even the happiest of marriages end in divorce. Having this deep subconscious belief and fear had me creating that in my life for the second time. But this time I knew what to do about it.

It would be over-simplifying it if I told you that changing that belief alone turned my marriage around. But I will say that using the techniques I'm going to tell you about later in this book did make me 100 percent committed to my marriage. In fact, the techniques I'm going to share with you made me feel happy in every area of my life.

Eventually I just couldn't help but to use these techniques on my clients. I was working at a clinic where alternative therapies are frowned upon, but I just couldn't help it. I felt like I had a magic wand and I wasn't allowed to use it. What I discovered was that my clients were getting better, and they were getting better fast. People started referring their friends to me.

In a very short amount of time, it became evident that the best thing for me to do was to go into private practice, where I could be honest about what I do and attract the clients who were ready for serious change. In a little more than a year, I had a waiting list.

It is a dream of mine to train therapists to incorporate the techniques I use into their therapy practices. But for now, my first step in sharing this with the world is to write this book. And honestly, if it saves just one marriage, it will be worth it to me.

Chapter 3:

Framework

*"You can't cross the sea merely by standing
and staring at the water."*
– Rabindranath Tagore

Tammy went to therapy to try to fix her marriage. Her therapist helped her realize that she didn't feel worthy of a healthy relationship. She started to see the correlation between never being good enough for her father and not feeling good enough for Chad. Her therapist asked her to start looking for evidence that she is worthy and good enough. Tammy tried really hard to find evidence to make her feel better, but the assignment seemed to backfire. Instead of finding evidence that she is worthy and good enough, Tammy found a ton of evidence that proved the opposite.

Tammy felt defeated. She continued to go to therapy for a short time, but knowing where her core beliefs came from didn't seem to help her feel better. She couldn't find evidence that they were not true despite her therapist's best efforts to help her do so. Now that she understood that she didn't feel good enough at her core, she had no idea how to change her feelings, so she gave up. She gave up on therapy and she felt like giving up on her marriage.

Does Tammy's story give you any ideas about what your core beliefs could be? Tammy couldn't figure out how to change them even with therapy, but there are ways to change them. I changed mine and now I am happy in my marriage. You can be happy again too.

You Can Do This

If you are feeling scared about your marriage right now, I completely understand. When I was feeling trapped, I would have given anything to save my marriage. I don't want you to have to feel like I felt. I chose to leave my marriage because I didn't know how to fix it, but I want you to feel like you have done everything you can to save your marriage before considering divorce. If you give up too easily, you might always wonder if you could have done more.

I wanted to write this book because I feel like I have discovered the secrets to healing any marriage that can possibly be healed. If you look at the statistics of couples who try marriage counseling that stay together, the numbers are grim. I can honestly say that most couples who have come to me have stayed together. Not only have they stayed together, but they have become really happy together again. I can only help a very small number of people in my private practice, but I feel compelled to share everything I know with as many people as I can reach. The divorce rate just shouldn't be so high. People give up way too soon. Don't become just another statistic.

What's Coming Next

In this book, I will continue to tell Tammy's story to show you how she let go of her limiting beliefs and started feeling happy in her marriage again. I will tell you how she did it without having to get Chad involved. By the end of this book, you will know how you can shift your marriage back in the right direction – just like Tammy did.

I will give you tangible things you can start doing right away to improve your marriage. You will have a new way to look at your partner and your marriage, so that your outlook can completely change. I will challenge you to look at where your views of marriage came from, so you can change the ones that are sabotaging you.

I have already given you the main reason why the passion in marriages usually fades. But I want you to understand the deeper reasons why marriages can fail because that is how I saved my current marriage. In the next chapter, I will give you some reasons I have seen that make people question their marriages.

Later in the book, I will go into detail about the technique that I came up with myself, which includes everything I've learned through my years of experience in working with clients. I will help you realize that you can heal at a deeper level than you ever imagined possible.

How to Use this Book

I recommend that you read this book all the way through the first time. Then I would go back and focus on Chapter 5. In that chapter, I give you things you can start doing right away. I give you some ideas for

writing techniques that can shift your mindset immediately. I would spend some time, at least a few weeks,
implementing these ideas into your life.

After taking a few weeks to implement the ideas
from Chapter 5, I suggest that you do the same with
Chapter 7, which is all about ways to revitalize your
life. If you are happy, you will have a much more positive energy, which will translate into a more optimistic
view of your marriage.

Marriage is something that is constantly growing
and changing. I once read a book called *The Marriage
Garden*. In it, they pose the question, *do you plant a
garden, then come back a few months later expecting to
be able to harvest the vegetables?* That always stuck with
me. Most people get married and do nothing to help
nurture their marriage or help it stay healthy. They do
nothing to work on it, yet they expect it to flourish. I
want you to use this book to learn how to make your
relationship grow.

I will help you understand that doing this work
on your marriage is important, and there are ways to
make it easier. I'm really excited to share this information with you, and I am hoping that it completely
changes your life. Are you ready to get started? I'll see
you in the next chapter.

Chapter 4:

Why Marriages Fail

*"Many people spend more time in
planning the wedding than they do in
planning the marriage."*
– Zig Ziglar

W hy do you think so many marriages end in divorce? Is everyone really just that bad at picking the right person?

When we first start dating someone, we only see the good things. Like I mentioned in Chapter 1, those chemicals that we call "love" make us stay in a constant state of bliss. Have you ever heard the expression "love is blind?" What happens is that we only see what we want to see at the beginning, and our partner is at his or her best, so they are only showing their best qualities. This is pretty easy when you are in a great mood all the time. Because we only know part of the story, we fill in the blanks of the other parts. Then, when things start to cool down, we start to see the truth of all the parts we filled in. We start to say things like "I don't know who he is anymore."

Resentment: The Relationship Killer

When most people start to see qualities in their partners that they don't like, they think their partners should change. Have you ever fixated on the things you'd like to change about your husband or wife? You think that if they would just change, then you would be happy. And how do you go about changing them? Normally people nag and point out the negative things, hoping it will motivate them to see what they are doing wrong. This almost never works, and if the person does end up changing for you, it leads to resentment.

You were probably taught that in order to make other people happy, you have to sacrifice and do things you don't want to do. If you don't do things to make other people happy, you are being selfish, right? The problem is that when you say "yes" when inside you are screaming "no," it leads to resentment. My therapist used to say, "Taking the best care of yourself is taking the best care of others." This is hard for most people to wrap their heads around, but if you do things that make you happy, you will have a more loving energy. When you are feeling good, you are more likely to want to do things for your partner. But this time you are doing it out of the energy of love rather than out of obligation.

Another thing that can lead to resentment is your differences in having or raising kids. Did you discuss whether or not you want kids with your spouse before you got married? I have been very surprised to find out how many couples never even broached the subject before they got married. If you did discuss it before marriage, did you discuss how many children you want? What about your parenting styles? If you got married assuming you were going to have a few kids and your partner doesn't want kids, it can be a huge problem. Either you give in and decide not to have kids, which leads to resentment, or they give in and have kids, which also leads to resentment. If you believe in spanking but your partner doesn't, it can cause problems. There are several scenarios related to this that can cause a marriage to end in divorce, but I think you get the point.

The Importance of Energy

Couples always come to me and say they are having marital problems and they need to work on their communication. I want you to understand that communication is not the actual problem. The actual problem is the lack of energy or feeling of connection between you. Think back to the beginning of your relationship when the energy between you was completely magnetic. How was your communication? It was easy, right? Now that being said, I will give you some ways to improve communication in your marriage, I just want you to understand that communication is a secondary problem.

Another thing people blame their problems on is their appearance. I have heard so many women tell me their husband is not attracted to her anymore because she has gained weight. Her husband may even believe that is true. But I want you to know the problem is not that she gained a few pounds. The problem is the lack of energy between them. I have had clients who were very thin and attractive who could never make a relationship work, and never got asked out. Then I've had clients who were overweight who had to beat the opposite sex off with a stick. It's all about energy and the way you feel about yourself.

Till Death Do Us Part "If" You Do What Makes Me Happy

When you got married, did you think your partner was going to make you happy? It is very common to think your marriage will make you feel that way. I mean, that is what happens in the movies, right? The fallacy in this is that, from the beginning, you have set your partner up to be loved conditionally. You will stay with them and love them as long as they continue to do things that make you happy, but you will leave if they start doing things that make you irritated or angry. Marriages cannot meet all of our needs or make us happy.

How would you rate your level of commitment to your partner right now? Since you are reading this book, I know you want to stay in your marriage, but how often do you consider leaving or getting a divorce? Or how often do you worry that your partner wants a divorce? A lack of commitment in a marriage feels completely unstable. It is very important that you decide you are "all in" before your relationship will feel safe and secure. I get that you are probably not there right now, but this book will help you see that it is possible to feel committed to your marriage again.

Feeling like You Married the Wrong Person

Many people come to me saying they are afraid they married the wrong person. When I ask them to tell me more, normally it becomes apparent that they don't know about the "love chemical." They think that because it went away, which it always does, it is evidence that there is someone else out there who they could keep that "in-love" feeling with long-term. Love changes over time, but it can get better when you get to know your partner on a deeper level.

If you can develop the long-lasting, deep love for your partner, when the spark shows back up, it is no longer the excitement that comes from the courtship phase of the relationship. But you can have times when those chemicals kick back in.

To get back to the story of Tammy, she thought Chad was her soul mate because she never had such strong feelings for anyone before. That is why she had no problem marrying him so soon. When these feelings went away, she thought that meant she was wrong about Chad, and that "the one" was still out there. But I'm here to tell you, "the one" is a myth. The truth is that we have several people on the planet we could be compatible and live a happy married life with.

The prospect that there is only one person we are destined to spend our life with is completely depressing *if* it doesn't end up working out. It can really set you back. I have many examples of this, but one that sticks out the most. Anna came to me after the death of her boyfriend. She just knew that he was her soul mate and now she was destined to be alone. She was depressed and had completely given up on the idea of having a family. It took her a while to get there, but now she is happily married with two kids. The reason I want you to understand this is because you may be thinking you were wrong about the person you married, so you need to leave them because "the one" is still out there. I'm here to tell you that is not the way it works.

Men vs. Women

Let's face it, men and women are just wired differently. One thing I have seen over and over is the differences in our views of sex. Men feel connected when they are having sex with their wives. I don't mean just during the act of sex, but if they have a healthy sex life, they generally feel happy in the relationship. Women want to feel connected before they desire sex. Do you see the disconnect here?

I had a client named Hadley. She had gone to a therapist to try to fix her marriage, but it didn't help. She said her therapist was a man, and he told her to start having sex with her husband more in order to save the marriage. He explained to her that her husband wasn't feeling connected because their sex life was suffering. Hadley said she tried to make herself have sex with her husband even though she wasn't feeling loved by him, but it wasn't sustainable. We had to do some deeper work before she was able to see improvements in her sex life and in her marriage.

I've given you some of the main reasons I've seen that have caused marriages to fail. If you have some of these problems, you may be feeling trapped or maybe you just feel like your marriage is doomed. But I want you to know that it is quite the opposite. There are deeper reasons for all of these problems and solutions to them as well. I want you to know that you can be happy again in this marriage. The next chapter will give you some tangible things you can start doing now to help.

Chapter 5:

Ways to Improve Your Marriage

*"When we seek to discover the best in others,
we somehow bring out the best in ourselves."*
– William Arthur Ward

Tammy thought that the only way to improve her marriage was for Chad to change some things she was not happy about. She nagged him and used passive-aggressive comments when he did something she didn't like.

She started reading a book on ways to improve her marriage. She began to realize that Chad didn't have to change a thing in order for her to be happy with him again. She realized that she had more control over the way she felt in her relationship than she previously understood.

The Power of Positive Thinking

There is a reason why you married the person you married. They have some qualities that you adore, even if you have lost sight of them. The first and most important thing I'm going to tell you is something that is going to become a theme of this book: *Start paying attention to the things you like about your partner and tell them.* If this is hard to get into your mind at the moment, take out a piece of paper and start writing all the things you like about your spouse. I promise you will come up with some things, and it will completely shift the way you feel.

Get to Know Your Partner on a Deeper Level

Do you feel like you know your husband or wife? What are their dreams and aspirations for the future? Where do they see themselves and you as a couple in 20 years? What would be their biggest dream come true? What is one of their favorite childhood memories? What did they dream of when they were a child? Do you know the answer to these questions? If you said "no," now might be a good time to ask.

This leads me to another important point: The biggest gift you can give your partner is to support their dreams. I know, I know, you probably don't feel supported right now either. But you have to take the first step. If you keep waiting for your partner to change or be supportive before you will be happy, you might be waiting a long time.

Start telling your partner what you like about them and start asking them questions right now. Get to know your him or her on a deeper level.

When they tell you their biggest aspirations and dreams, it is very important that you listen without judgment. For example, my husband has a dream of quitting his job, buying a big sailboat and sailing around the world. I have not always been supportive of that dream because we have a daughter who is in school, I have a job I love, we own a house, etc. I have scoffed at the idea of picking up everything and sailing around the world. But I have to let him have his dream. Now when I visualize us way in the future, I keep seeing us on a boat in the Caribbean. How great is that! Nurture your partner's dreams.

Love Languages

Do you know your partner's love language? Most people don't even know what that means, but it is very important. There is a book called *The Five Love Languages*. In it, the authors explain that there are different ways people feel and express their love. The first one is *words of affirmation*. This is exactly what I was talking about earlier. Some people feel loved when you notice the good things they are doing or their positive qualities, and you tell them about it. People also tend to express their love for you according to their main love language.

The second love language is *gifts*. A person whose love language is *gifts* feels love when they receive a gift, and they show their love by giving gifts. This doesn't mean that they have to receive expensive gifts all the time, but just buying them something thoughtful once in a while can go a long way.

The third love language is *physical touch*. This is not necessarily sex, but just physical affection such as cuddling, holding hands, getting massaged, etc. When this is someone's love language, you might be surprised at how much a relationship will improve if they regularly receive loving hugs from their partner.

The fourth love language is *quality time*. In this one, the most important thing is spending time doing things together. It doesn't mean that you have to spend all of your time together. In fact, it is healthy to have your own interests and hobbies that are separate from your partner's. But spending time together doing something that you both enjoy is important even if it is not your first love language.

The last love language is *acts of service*. When someone's love language is acts of service, they feel loved when their partner does things for them like cleaning the house, washing their car, or mowing the lawn. This one can often be easily misinterpreted. If your partner gets mad because they don't feel like you have done enough around the house, it can trigger something inside you that makes you mad as well. Your feelings about that might change if you realize that he or she is only acting that way because it is their love language.

After reading the five love languages, which one or ones most resonate with you? What makes you feel loved and how do you express your love? Which one do you think is your partner's?

I have some clients, Tracy and John, who have different love languages and it has caused some problems. Tracy's love language is physical touch. She feels loved when she gets to cuddle with John, hold hands, etc. John's love language is acts of service, so he feels loved when Tracy washes the dishes or makes the bed. Before they came to see me, Tracy would complain that the only time she ever got physical attention from John is when they were having sex. She would try to hold hands with him and curl up with him to watch a movie, but John either didn't seem interested or he took it as an advancement toward sex. Since John's love language is acts of service, he would complain when he got home and the house was a mess. This made Tracy angry, and normally started an argument. In order to make it up to Tracy, John would wash her car or mow the lawn, but he never got the acknowledgment he was expecting when he did these things for her.

Does it seem clear how Tracy and John are *missing the mark* with each other? When I explained the love languages to them, it changed everything. Tracy started to realize that John was not as old-fashioned as she thought, just wanting her to clean the house because she was a woman. She started being more mindful of getting things done around the house because she knew it made John feel loved. Then when John came home and the house was clean, he automatically became more affectionate.

When John realized that Tracy felt loved when he held her hand or gave her a back rub, he made a conscious effort to be more affectionate. The more he was physically affectionate with her, the more she wanted to do things for him. Then without even working on it directly, it completely turned their sex life around because they both started feeling important and loved.

If you don't know your or your partner's love languages, there is a free online quiz you can take to find out (http://www.5lovelanguages.com/profile/couples/). It is also a fun way of bringing up ways to improve your marriage, and let your partner know that they are important to you.

Communication Styles

Since everyone wants to talk about it, I feel compelled to tell you more about communication. The first thing you need to know is that there are four different communication styles. I'm going to briefly explain them, then I will go into more detail. There is passive, where you don't communicate your needs or desires, and possibly let other people walk all over you. If someone who is passive never lets their feelings out in some way, it can literally make them sick. The second communication style is aggressive, where you communicate your needs loudly, and you don't take the other person's feelings into consideration. Then there is passive-aggressive, where you manipulate the other person in an effort to get your needs met. The last communication style is assertive, where you openly and honestly express your desires and ask for what you need, while also being considerate of the other person's feelings.

Which communication style sounds the healthiest to you? Which communication style do you think you and your partner use most often? Assertiveness is the thing we should all strive for, but it's not always easy if you have a long history of communicating in a different way.

Going back to John and Tracy, how do you think John could most effectively get Tracy to help him with the dishes? If he were being passive, he would not say anything about it and he would just do it himself. The problem with this lack of communication is that it leads to resentment. He is most likely stewing inside and is definitely not putting out a loving energy toward Tracy. If he were being aggressive, he would yell at her and tell her she needs to help him *right now* because he is getting angry. If he were being passive-aggressive, he would say something like, "You never help me with the dishes." Using any of these communication styles will most likely lead to an argument, either immediately or down the road.

How could John communicate assertively in this situation? He could say, "Tracy, would you please help me with the dishes?" It sounds simple, right? Start paying attention to you and your partner's styles; if you are having problems, you might not be using the assertive communication style very often.

What about when there is something bothering you that you feel you need to discuss with your partner? What communication style do you use then? When do you bring it up? Most people wait until they *can't take it anymore* and they end up trying to discuss it when they are in the middle of the problem. Even if you tend to use another communication style more often, you can get aggressive when you feel like you have had enough. The problem with getting aggressive is obvious, but how could you do it differently?

A very important thing to remember is to *bring up the problem at a neutral time*. If you discuss things right when you are in the middle of the problem, you are likely to be angry, and it will almost always lead to an argument.

Let's say John wants to talk to Tracy about the fact that he feels like he always has to do all the chores around the house. He gets home from work on a day when Tracy has been at home all day and the house is a mess. He ends up yelling at Tracy, and saying, "What have you been doing all day? The house is a mess!" How well do you think this is going to go over?

A better way looks something like this: John and Tracy are eating dinner together, and John says he wants to talk about the fact that they seem to have a hard time keeping the house clean. He tells Tracy he knows the amount of work that needs to be done around the house can be overwhelming, and he asks her for suggestions that would make it easier for them to get it done together.

This leads to another important point. If John asks Tracy to help him do the dishes and Tracy is in the middle of something important to her, what do you think would be her best response? We are taught to put other people first and to sacrifice for our partners, right? So, if she stops doing something that is important to her and helps him with the dishes even though she is screaming *no* inside, what do you think will happen over time? Remember, saying yes when you really mean no leads to resentment. That is not to say that Tracy should just let John do all the chores and never help with the dishes. Something that would work better is if she would say something like, "John, I know it is important to you that I help with the dishes. Right now, I am in the middle of something that is important to me. How about you wash the dishes now and when I'm finished I will dry them and put them away?" Then John gets what he wants, and Tracy helps John in a way that doesn't create resentment.

Some people check in at the end of each day to see how the other person's day went. This is a good thing to do, but let me tell you how it can go wrong. Let's say Tracy had a disagreement with a co-worker and she wants to tell John about it. What do you think she wants from him when she tells John about how things happened and how angry she is feeling? John's instinct is to give her advice about how she could resolve this issue with her co-worker. Does this sound familiar? John is absolutely doing his best to be supportive, but he is completely missing the mark with Tracy. What she actually needs is for him to listen and be empathetic. A more supportive response would be, "Wow Tracy, it sounds like you had a hard day. I bet you were feeling really angry when she did that." Then if Tracy asks for advice on how to solve the problem, by all means give her advice. But don't give advice to your partner unless they ask for it.

Nurture Your Relationship and Yourself

Remember, "Taking the best care of yourself is taking the best care of others." This means that you should take time to nurture yourself and do things that you love. This ties into saying "yes" when you really mean "no." It has been ingrained in us that if we do not make sacrifices for other people we are being selfish. But, as you can see in the example with Tracy and John, making the sacrifice can lead to resentment. Think about it this way: When are you in the best mood? When you have been doing something you love, right? If you have the day off and you clean the house all day because that is what your husband wants you to do, how do you feel when he gets home from work? But what if you go to a yoga class and have lunch with a friend? Afterward you might feel like spending some time cleaning the house because you know it is important to your husband. Then when he gets home you can greet him with love rather than anger. I will get more into the how of taking the best care of yourself in Chapter 7.

Being present with your partner can greatly improve your relationship. Remember that it is important to spend quality time together even if it is not your first love language. How often do you sit and talk or even watch a movie together without getting on your phone, iPad, or reading a book? I have seen some couples where the absolute biggest problem they have is that one or both of them is constantly on social media. It is definitely okay to have some times when you are not engaged with each other, but it is not okay for it to be all the time. Put the phone down! Talk to your partner!

This chapter is important so let me review:

- Ask questions to get to know your partner better
- Support your partner's life dreams (even if you think they are unrealistic)
- Pay attention to the things you like about your partner and tell them
- Know and be mindful of your partner's love languages
- Take the best care of yourself so that you want to take the best care of your partner
- Bring up problems at a neutral time and be assertive
- Spend time connecting with your partner without any distractions such as your phone
- Be empathetic rather than giving advice

Chapter 6:

The Law of Attraction

"Whatever you hold in your mind on a consistent basis is exactly what you will experience in your life."
– Tony Robbins

Once upon a time there were two women who had very similar lives and were married to very similar men. One day God came down and asked each woman to tell him about how things were going in her marriage.

The first woman said, "Things are terrible. My husband is so busy with work that he never pays attention to me. He works at a dead-end job and we can barely make ends meet. I have to stay home with the kids all day because we can't afford to put them in daycare, and if I worked, it wouldn't even cover the cost of child care. Every day is exactly the same miserable day and I feel completely trapped in this marriage and in this life." Then God said to her, "You think that's bad! I'll show you bad!"

The second woman told God, "My life is wonderful! I feel so blessed to have a husband who goes to work every day to provide for our family. We don't get much time together, but we try to make the most of the time we do have. I am so grateful that I get to spend this time at home with my children and watch them grow up during these important years. I wouldn't change a thing." Then God said to her, "You think that is good! I'll show you good!"

Universal Laws

There are universal laws that people rarely talk about and you never learned in school. The first one is the Law of Vibration. All we are is energy, and everything and everyone is vibrating at a certain frequency. We can't see it with the naked eye, so most people are unaware of it. When you are vibrating at a very low frequency, you feel anxious, depressed, angry, nervous, etc. When you are vibrating at a high frequency, you feel joyful. I'm going to talk more about energy in Chapter 9.

Another universal law is the Law of Attraction. This law states that the more you pay attention to something, the more it will come into your existence. So, when you pay attention to things you like, more things you like will show up in your life. But when you pay attention to things you don't like, you will see more things you don't like. Worrying is like creating something you don't want. Have you ever heard of self-fulfilling prophecy? It's actually a real phenomenon because you bring negative things into your existence by your attention to them.

Remember the parenting intervention I taught at the beginning of my career? I told you that The Attention Principle worked, and by the end of the book you would know why. Let me explain in the context of the Law of Attraction.

Katie had a ten-year-old son named Bruce. Bruce never did what Katie told him to do, including his chores. He often talked back to his mom and she thought he was so disrespectful. Every chance she got, Katie told Bruce he was lazy and inconsiderate. She repeatedly asked him to do his chores, and when he didn't respond, she would repeat herself over and over until she got angry. Then she would start to yell, and she would say things that she later regretted. What do you think is going on here? The Incredible Years' explanation would be that she is reinforcing Bruce's negative behavior, so the negative behavior is increasing. This is true, and the Law of Attraction is also at play.

The more you pay attention to something, even if it is just in your thoughts, the more you will see it. This is true because the universe responds to your vibration. If you are thinking things that make you feel angry, you have a strong vibration related to the subject. The universe responds to the strong vibration and brings more of it into your experience.

Let's say Katie starts to pay attention to Bruce when he is doing something she likes, and she praises him. If Bruce makes his bed one day and she tells him how happy that makes her, Bruce is more likely to make the bed the next day as well. Does this sound familiar? It also works with husbands and wives! Katie is positively reinforcing Bruce's good behavior, and she is also feeling good about it. So, when she is in the energy and vibration of appreciation, she will see more of that behavior.

Appreciation and Visualization

When you make a list of all of the things you appreciate about your partner, it makes you feel more loving and appreciative of them. If you can get in the habit of noticing the good things and ignoring the bad, you will feel better. If you start feeling happy, more things that make you happy will come into your existence. It is universal law!

I want you to think of the things you want right now. You are reading this book, so I know you want to have a happy, healthy marriage. Think about how you want things to be different in your life. Do your desires feel good to you?

If you can think about your marriage in an optimistic, dreamy type of a state, you are in the right energy to attract improvements. If you can visualize yourself a year from now, feeling happy that you have solved this problem and seeing yourself in the energy of appreciation for your marriage and your partner, you're on the right track.

But what if you just don't really think it's possible to be happy in your marriage again? What if you try to think of yourself in a fulfilling marriage but it just reminds you that you are not feeling that way now and it makes you sad? If this is the case, you are in the energy of lack. When you are in this energy, improvement in your marriage is *not* on its way.

So how do you get from the energy of lack regarding your marriage to an energy of manifesting a healthy marriage? One way is visualization. Close your eyes and think of a time when you and your partner had a great time together. Get in touch with that memory with all of your senses. See it, feel it, smell it, taste it, and hear it. Then imagine yourself in the future having a great time with your partner. Again, get into it with all of your senses. If you can feel it before it comes into your life, it is on its way! Keep it up!

I have already mentioned that getting out a piece of paper and writing everything you like about your partner is a good way to shift your energy about them. You can also make it a daily practice by starting an appreciation journal. You can use this to make yourself feel happier in every area of your life, and while you are working on improving your marriage, you may want to just start with writing what you appreciate about your partner. You can do this anytime, day or night. One time that works really well is right before you go to bed. If you do this, you will get a better night's sleep, have more pleasant dreams, and wake up in a better mood. It doesn't even matter if you just say the same things over and over. In fact, that is actually a positive thing because it trains your brain to notice those things throughout the day.

Vision Boards

If you have a hard time seeing it in your mind, another option is to use a vision board. Cut pictures that make you feel happy and inspired out of a magazine. Glue them to a poster board and either put it where you can see it, or pull it out and look at it every day. Get into the feeling of already having the things in the pictures. If you are working on your marriage, you might cut out a picture of a couple having a candlelit dinner together, a picture of two people getting a couples' massage, and a picture of a couple holding hands at the beach. As you look at the pictures, get into the joyful feelings that come up. Remember, the universe responds to the way you feel. If you can get into the feeling of having a healthy relationship, a fulfilling and joyful relationship is headed your way.

One of my favorite stories about the way a vision board worked for someone is something I saw on You-Tube. Someone was interviewing a Law of Attraction guy named John Assaraf as they were sitting by his beautiful pool in California. John was saying that several years ago, he had a vision board that he looked at regularly. Then he moved to a new office, packed up his stuff, and didn't unpack the vision board. He said he then moved to California and bought the house where they were filming the video. After the move, he came across the box with his vision board in it. When he pulled it out and looked at the house he had put on it, there was a picture of not just a similar house to the one he bought, but it was *the exact* house and he didn't even realize it! I love that story because it so easily illustrates the concept of using the Law of Attraction to manifest anything you want.

Release Resistance to Improve Your Feelings

> *"If you knew your potential to feel good, you would ask no one to be different so that you can feel good. You would free yourself of all of that cumbersome impossibility of needing to control the world, or control your mate, or control your child. You are the only one who creates your reality. For no one else can think for you, no one else can do it. It is only you, every bit of it you."*
> – Abraham-Hicks

A good resource for learning more about the Law of Attraction is Abraham-Hicks. There are many books by Ester and Jerry Hicks and YouTube videos if you want to learn more.

Our natural state is to feel good. Instead of trying to make things happen the way you want them to happen, let go of resistance to your natural, good-feeling state and you will feel some relief. There is an analogy that Abraham-Hicks gives of a cork in the water. The extent to which you are not feeling good is the extent to which you are resisting your natural state, which is like holding a cork underwater. If you would just let go of resistance or let go of the cork and let it float up to the top of the water, you would feel happy. How are you resisting your natural state in your marriage?

When I first learned about the Law of Attraction, it totally freaked me out. I would be walking around and when I noticed that I was having a negative thought, I would panic because I knew I was attracting more negative things into my life. At the end of the book *Ask and It Is Given* by Ester and Jerry Hicks, it gives many different techniques you can use to start manifesting the life you desire. I started doing many of the techniques I learned in the book. The techniques were definitely helpful, and I did feel better, but I didn't really start becoming a great manifestor until I started using the techniques that I will talk about in Chapter 9. If this concept freaks you out too, stick with me because I have ways to make it easier.

Chapter 7:

Creating the Life You Want

"If you look at what you have in life, you'll always have more. If you look at what you don't have in life, you'll never have enough."
– Oprah Winfrey

Tammy spent a lot of time thinking about the changes she needed Chad to make so their marriage could improve. She wanted him to spend more time engaging with her after work rather than getting on his iPad or watching TV. She wanted him to eat healthier because it was so hard for her to lose weight when he eats anything he wants. She wanted him to start helping more with the household chores. She wanted more physical affection.

Tammy had a co-worker named Elizabeth who always seemed happy, and always had good things to say about her husband and her marriage. One day when they were talking, Tammy told Elizabeth she must feel really lucky that she met the perfect man and therefore her marriage is so easy. Elizabeth told her that her marriage has not been without its problems, but they have both worked on themselves and things have gotten much better. Tammy was confused but intrigued by the concept of working on yourself to make your marriage better. She asked Elizabeth what she could do to work on herself. Elizabeth told her that there are a lot of things, but the first place she would start is to meditate for 15 minutes a day. Elizabeth didn't give her any rules, but just said to shut her eyes and set the timer on her phone.

Tammy decided to take Elizabeth's advice. After all, she could definitely spare 15 minutes a day and she didn't have anything to lose. Tammy found it very difficult at first and thought the time just seemed to drag. But she stuck with it and found that it got much easier.

Tammy was meditating just 15 minutes each morning, but she started to notice that it really shifted her mood throughout the day. Something else happened that she wasn't expecting: she stopped feeling annoyed when Chad came home and got on his iPad. She had a more loving energy toward him, and he started engaging with her more and more. She started feeling connected to him again, and sometimes even had a feeling like she was in love with life when she was with him. She also stopped blaming him for the fact that she couldn't lose weight, and she stopped being so mean to herself. Eventually she noticed that she was feeling happier on more of a consistent basis, her marriage was looking better every day, and she even dropped a few pounds without trying.

Besides meditating, Tammy started spending time outside of work with Elizabeth. They went to yoga classes, had lunch, and started walking together. Tammy realized that she had never been around anyone who was so positive. In the past, she always sat around complaining about her husband and all the things that were not working out in her life. But Elizabeth seemed to bring out the best in her. She found herself talking about the improvements she had been seeing in her marriage and her life. After spending time with Elizabeth, she felt uplifted and optimistic about her future. When she went home, she noticed that she and Chad got along better.

Change Yourself to Improve Your Relationship

Do you ever find yourself thinking about the things your partner needs to change so that your marriage will improve? If the answer is yes, don't feel bad because almost everyone does. But you cannot do anything to change your partner, and your attention to the things you want to change magnifies them and makes you unhappy. The good news is that you can change the way you feel right now by paying attention to the positive aspects of your partner. As you read in Chapter 6, the Law of Attraction is always working. When you pay attention to the positive things in your life, you feel better, and the universe responds by bringing more positive things into your life.

For many years I explored self-help techniques, and I dabbled in several of them. They did make me feel better, but only up to a point. Then something I read in a Jack Kornfield book really resonated with me, and it changed my life. He said that there are many techniques you can use to make yourself more balanced and happier, but it is very important that you pick one and stick with it. He said the mistake many people make is trying to do too much, which makes them not stick to any one thing, so they never actually receive the full benefits.

The other thing that I want you to think about is that it is important to start doing something as a daily practice. I have seen many people who learn techniques, but plan to use them only when something bad happens and they are right in the middle of it. The problem with this is that they forget to do it when they are right in the middle of the problem. Consider this: Do people who are going to run a marathon start running on the day of the race? Of course, this would not result in finishing the marathon. They have to train for several months, then they are ready on the day of the race. It is the same thing with starting a daily practice that will help you feel happier. When a new problem arises, your daily practice becomes your "go to" to help you feel better.

Meditation

One technique you could start right away is meditation. Like Tammy, you might find that it improves your mood and your marriage. The best time to meditate is right when you get up in the morning, but it would be beneficial to do it at any time of the day. There are several ways to do meditation, but you can just do what Tammy did, which is close your eyes and set a timer for 15 minutes. Paying attention to your breath or a sound in the room can be helpful. I know 15 minutes doesn't seem like a lot of time, but many people find it very difficult at first. If you are one of those people, know that it gets easier and just keep doing it.

If you find it too difficult to start meditating on your own, there are many mediation apps you can download on your phone or computer. Some of them have music, guided visualizations or just someone instructing you to keep focusing your attention on your breath. After I read the Jack Kornfield book I mentioned earlier, I decided to invest in a meditation program called Centerpointe, which uses Holosync technology to change your brain waves. It is more of a time commitment because it is a one-hour meditation, but I would highly recommend it. They say the best time to do it is right when you wake up or in the middle of the day, but I would go to bed early and listen to it in bed. By the time it ended, I was ready to sleep like a baby. This program comes with a book that will explain what is happening to your brain when you listen to the meditation with headphones. The short explanation is that it balances the left and right hemispheres of your brain by creating new neuropathways.

If an hour seems like way too much of a commitment but you want to use a technology that will automatically put you in a deeper brainwave state, look for a meditation that uses binaural beats. Binaural beats automatically put your brain in the Theta brainwave. This is the brainwave you are in during hypnosis and a brainwave you will get in during meditation once you have been practicing it a while.

Your brain does not normally go into the Theta brainwave unless you are sleeping. Going into the Theta brainwave causes you to feel very relaxed and rejuvenated. It decreases depression and anxiety, improves memory, and calms the mind. It helps you fall asleep easier and have a deeper, more peaceful sleep so that you wake up feeling refreshed in the morning. It causes your body to release hormones that increase health and longevity. If you want to read more about the benefits of the Theta brainwave or binaural beats meditations, you can find a ton of information online.

Another type of meditation that can be very peaceful is called a loving-kindness meditation. You can find a guided one, but the idea of it is simple. You start by closing your eyes and focusing on the love you feel in your heart. Sometimes it helps to think of a person or place you love the most. Then you imagine that the love you feel in your heart is expanding with every heartbeat, out into your entire body. Then you expand the love into the whole room. You expand the love out into the entire house or building, then the entire city. You expand the love out into the entire state, the entire country, the entire continent, then out to the entire Earth. Lastly, you expand the love out to the entire Universe. This process only takes a few minutes, but you can sit in the loving energy for as long as you like. Imagine how peaceful the world would be if everyone did a loving-kindness meditation every day.

Movement to Improve Your Energy

If the thought of sitting quietly just does not appeal to you, you might want to try Qigong (or Chi-Gong), which combines body movement, breathing, and meditating. I have heard that it can be very complex, but I learned a version that is quite simple called Spring Forest Qigong. You can buy a video and follow along until you learn the entire sequence. Starting a daily Qigong practice will have similar benefits to sitting meditation. You will feel more balanced, less stressed, and just generally happier. When I was practicing this on a regular basis, if I came home in a bad mood, my husband would say, "You didn't do Qigong today, did you?" He was almost always right!

Tap out Your Negative Emotions

Another technique you can learn and start using to feel better right away is EFT (Emotional Freedom Technique) or tapping. I am going to warn you that this technique feels very silly, but doing it can completely change your life, so it's worth it. When you do this technique, you focus on something that is upsetting to you while you tap on meridian points on the top half of your body. It seems too good to be true, but what happens is that whatever you are focusing on loses its emotional charge. In other words, it no longer upsets you, and it only takes a few minutes. But the best part about it is that when you "tap something out," your feelings about it are actually gone *forever*. My clients don't usually believe me until they leave my office and realize they really are not upset about it anymore at all.

I was doing this way before I really understood how it works, but now I have a scientific explanation for it. When you are thinking about something that upsets you, your body secretes cortisol (the stress hormone) and adrenaline. When you start tapping on these very specific meridian points while continuing to focus on the same subject, it signals your brain that you are safe, and your body starts secreting dopamine and serotonin. Your brain starts to make a connection between the negative thought and safety, which creates a new neuropathway in your brain. This makes the negative emotional charge completely go away.

If you are interested in learning more about this technique, you can find information online. One great source is *The Tapping Solution*. I also highly recommend looking up Brad Yates on YouTube and following along with one of his many tapping videos. I often recommend that my clients do Brad's videos called "tap o' the mornin'" and "tap o' the evenin.'" The first one helps you tap out any reason why you wouldn't have a great day, and the second one helps you tap out any negative thing that happened that day, so you can let it go.

Limit Your Time Watching the News

Another thing I highly recommend is to limit the amount of time you watch the news and pay attention to social media regarding all the bad things that are happening in our world. Watching the news keeps everyone in a constant state of fight or flight. Our world is not actually as bad as they portray in the news, but the news gives all its attention to the negative things that are happening. This trains your mind to only focus on the bad things in your life.

Take a moment to consider the implications of the fact that everyone is paying attention to the traumatic events in our world. Remember the Law of Attraction? It also ties into something I will explain in the next chapter, which is the collective consciousness. We are all plugged into a fear-based mentality because that is what is portrayed on the news. I know, I know … we have to stay informed, right? That is something that was ingrained into me by my parents, so I know you might have similar beliefs. But I challenge you to greatly limit or turn off the news for just a couple of weeks and see if you start feeling happier. The fact that so many people are plugged into the fear is actually the thing that keeps so many negative things happening in the world.

Taking Care of Yourself Could Save Your Marriage

How does it make you feel to think of taking more time for yourself? Like I have mentioned in previous chapters, we are taught that we have to spend more time taking care of other people or we are being selfish.

Some of my clients have a really hard time unlearning what their parents and the world have taught them about being selfish. But the truth is, if you put yourself first, you will be happy. If you are happy, you put a more loving energy into everything you do, which makes you put more loving energy into your interactions with your husband or wife. When you put out a more loving energy, you have a healthier marriage. This is not the same as spending more time with your spouse. If you spend less time with them, but the time spent is coming from a more loving energy, it will have much more benefit to both of you than if you spend more time with a resentful energy.

Let Down Your Wall

How would it make you feel if I asked you to start being more vulnerable? That word used to have a strong negative charge for me and several of my clients. But vulnerability has gotten a bad rap. When you let down your wall and allow yourself to be vulnerable with your partner, it allows you to feel closer and more connected. If you have a hard time with this concept, which I imagine you do, I recommend watching Brené Brown's Ted Talk on vulnerability. You would also likely benefit from some deeper work regarding the subject, which I will talk about in the next two chapters.

Here are some things to remember about this chapter:

- Choose a daily practice that resonates with you and make it a priority in your life
- Focus on the positive things in your life and talk with people about them
- Redefine the word "selfish" for yourself and start putting yourself first
- Limit time watching the news and/or focusing on the media
- Let down your wall and allow yourself to be more vulnerable (and maybe do deeper work on this one)

Chapter 8:

Subconscious Mind

*"If we could get your subconscious mind
to agree with your conscious mind
about being happy, that's when your
positive thoughts work."*
— Bruce Lipton

Beliefs Are Programmed in Childhood

At the beginning of the book I talked about my parents' marriage and divorce. I always believed they were in a happy marriage. Therefore, when they got divorced, I developed the belief that even happy marriages end in divorce. But what I didn't explain is that I didn't even know I had that belief. In other words, it wasn't a conscious belief. Through the years I have talked to both my mom

71

and my dad about their marriage, and they have both shared things that made me understand their relationship definitely had its problems. They were just really good at hiding it. But when I started digging into my beliefs, the belief was there on a subconscious level.

Your subconscious mind is like the hard drive of a computer. It records everything that ever happens to you and is responsible for 95 percent of what is going on with you, yet you are not consciously aware of it. Since you are unaware of it, I bet you are wondering where it comes from and how you can find out what subconscious beliefs could be sabotaging your marriage.

Tammy grew up in a family where her mother was emotionally unavailable, and her father was abusive. Her parents didn't interact with each other often, much less show affection, and when they did interact it was normally during an argument. In early childhood, Tammy developed a subconscious belief that marriages lack love and affection. As she got older, she just knew she could have a relationship that was different than her parents'. However, her subconscious beliefs put her right in the middle of an unhappy marriage.

The main place where your subconscious beliefs come from is early childhood. The scary thing is that you didn't choose any of them. They were programmed into you by your parents, siblings, teachers, friends, TV, church, the internet, and just being out in the world. Young children are like little sponges, taking in everything they observe and hear. By the time you are six or seven, most of your beliefs are solidly locked into place, and it takes a lot to change them.

Remember Katie from chapter 6? Until she took the parenting class, she constantly told her son Bruce he was lazy and inconsiderate. It was basically like she downloaded those beliefs right into him. What beliefs do you think your parents programmed into you that could be negatively affecting your relationship?

I had a client named Ellen who came to me because she was having problems in her marriage. She told me her husband just didn't find her attractive anymore, which she said was evidenced by their suffering sex life. When we dug into it more, she had a subconscious belief that no one could ever love her because she was fat. But the thing was, Ellen was not even one-pound overweight. When I asked her about it, she said she knew she wasn't overweight in her head, but she always felt fat and unattractive. We discovered that these beliefs came from her sister, because her sister always told Ellen she was fat, ugly, and no one would ever love her.

Once we discovered Ellen's subconscious beliefs and changed them, she reported that her sex life and connection with her husband improved almost immediately. Though I never actually met her husband, Ellen told me he jokingly said he was going to send me flowers! Ellen didn't actually have a weight problem, but I do feel compelled to mention again that weight is never the actual problem in relationships. It's all about confidence and the way you feel about yourself, which is directly related to your subconscious beliefs.

Beliefs Are Passed Down in Your Genes

"Honestly, sometimes I get really fed up of my subconscious – it's like it's got a mind of its own."
– Alexei Sayle

Do you have any fears that don't make sense, like a fear of driving when you have never been in a car accident? One reason this can happen is because subconscious beliefs and traumas can be passed down genetically. In fact, in a research study by Dias and Ressler, male mice were mildly shocked while being exposed to the scent of cherry blossom. The male mice were then bred with females, and the baby mice had trauma reactions to the scent of cherry blossom even though they had never been exposed to the scent previously.

A man named Paul came to me because he had a phobia of leaving the house. When we discussed it more, he said he was okay when he was with his wife or anyone else, but he felt panicked if he tried to go anywhere alone. When I tapped into it, he had a genetic trauma that was passed down from his mother where she was left alone in the crib when she was very young. We cleared the trauma and beliefs associated with it, and Paul only had to see me that one time. He reported that the phobia, which had been getting worse over the years, completely disappeared after that session.

What genetic beliefs about marriage do you think you have that were passed down from your parents, grandparents, or even several generations back?

Susie came to me because she had been in several abusive relationships. She said every time she started dating, she swore she would never date another abusive man, but she would find out they were abusive several months into the relationship. She even married a man that later became abusive.

Why would someone attract abuse over and over? We discovered that Susie had several beliefs such as "All men are abusive" and "I deserve to be abused" on the genetic level. In other words, one of her relatives had been abused, had developed these beliefs, and passed them down to Susie. After we worked on all of these beliefs, she attracted a very nice man. They later got married, and Susie reports that they are very happy.

Beliefs Come from Past Lives

Another place where people have developed sub-conscious beliefs that don't make sense is past lives. When I was in graduate school, I was interested in the concept of past lives, so my friend told me to read the book *Many Lives, Many Masters* by Brian Weiss. Dr. Weiss is a psychiatrist who had a client he calls Kath-erine. He reported that Katherine had severe anxiety and was not responding to traditional therapy, so he decided to hypnotize her to explore the possibility that a repressed trauma could be causing her symptoms. First, she did remember repressed sexual abuse from this life, but the discovery did not help her symptoms. Dr. Weiss regressed her again, and this time when he asked her to go back to where her symptoms origi-nated, she spontaneously went back to a past life. In the book, he recalls that they were both pretty freaked out and did not believe in past lives previously. How-ever, they were so intrigued that he regressed her to dozens of past lives and recorded the sessions. Years later, when he decided to share the information, he put direct quotes from Katherine's regressions in the book. He reported that she knew historical information that she had no knowledge of in this life, and at one point, she was even speaking another language. The other thing he discovered is that Katherine's symptoms subsided after she became aware of their origins under hypnosis.

Honestly when I read *Many Lives, Many Masters* I couldn't put it down. I read several of his books, and they changed my life. The recurring message is "Only love is real," and that is actually the title of one of Dr. Weiss's books. Soon after graduate school, I trained in hypnosis, and later attended a training by Brian Weiss where I learned how to do past life regressions.

Ray and Trisha came to me because they were having problems in their marriage. They had been together for many years and had recently been having problems. Trisha was holding onto resentment from their newlywed days, it had been festering, and she had an affair. When Ray found out about the affair, he was livid, to say the least. I helped him release his anger and helped her clear her resentment, but she still wasn't sure if she wanted to stay in the marriage. Through the course of therapy, Ray discovered that he had not been emotionally available in the relationship, and he wanted nothing more than to make their marriage work despite the affair.

Ray and Trisha's relationship improved slightly, but things didn't improve significantly until we made a discovery regarding a past life. In that life they were also married, and Ray was extremely physically abusive, which eventually led to Trisha's death. Becoming aware of that helped us discover that Trisha was holding onto a feeling and belief that she had to punish Ray for what he had done to her in that life. When I released the trauma and associated beliefs, their marriage immediately improved.

When beliefs and traumas are discovered from past lives, typically my clients say that something about it seems to resonate with them. For example, even though Trisha had forgiven Ray for some indiscretions that occurred early in their marriage, she said she did have a feeling that she still needed to punish him for something. Ray agreed that it felt like Trisha had been punishing him much more harshly than he felt he deserved from anything he had done in this life.

The Collective Consciousness

Another place where subconscious beliefs come from is the collective or group consciousness. These are beliefs that a large number of people are plugged into, so most people would define the beliefs as fact. An example of this would be the aging process. Most people believe that when we get old we get wrinkles, grey hair, our bones get brittle, we become hunched over, we lose or gain weight, we become less mobile … I think I could go on and on. But what if those things were true only because we believe they are true? I know this one is hard to believe, but those things do not have to happen to us just because we get older. Have you ever known an old person who has more energy and looks better than someone 30 years younger than them? Have you ever heard you are only as old as you think you are or only as old as you feel? This is literally true.

When my daughter was six years old, she broke her collar bone. I have never been an overprotective mother, but all of the sudden I was hovering over her telling her to be careful all the time. I was terrified that she would re-injure herself and need surgery. I knew that was the wrong energy to put out toward her, but I literally couldn't make myself stop.

I even tried all of my healing techniques and nothing would make it go away. I had to call on another healer who I knew could help me figure it out. He said I had plugged into the helicopter parenting collective consciousness. When he unplugged me, I was completely calm around my daughter from that moment forward.

Abandonment and Absorption

The two most common subconscious fears in relationships are the fear of abandonment and the fear of absorption. If you are unaware of them, and do nothing to heal them, these fears could sabotage your marriage.

People can develop the fear of abandonment very easily. For example, I have many clients who didn't grow up in the house with both parents. Some of them didn't have contact with the parent who didn't raise them, which leads them to feel abandoned. It is easy to see where you could develop the fear and belief that your partner is going to abandon you if that is what you witnessed in childhood. But what about your previous relationships? This doesn't even have to be with a romantic partner. It could be a friend who decided they no longer wanted to hang out with you.

There are hundreds of ways you could develop the fear of abandonment.

The fear of absorption means that you fear you will lose your sense of self in a relationship. So, you are afraid that you will no longer be able to be yourself, and function as an independent person. In other words, you may not know who you are anymore if you stay in the relationship.

Many people have the fear of abandonment or the fear of absorption on a conscious level. But if you don't have one or both on a conscious level, there is a huge chance that you have at least one of them on a subconscious level because of all the different places these fears and beliefs come from.

So how do these subconscious fears show up in relationships? One way is that, when you start to feel close to someone, it feels unsafe, so you pull away. This keeps you from developing a deep connection with people, and you wouldn't even be aware that you are doing it. It could cause you to feel so disconnected in your marriage that you end up getting a divorce. If you are not the one doing this, it could be your partner. Either way, the relationship can only go so deep if one or both of you are experiencing these subconscious fears.

Muscle Testing

Are you are wondering what beliefs and fears you have on a subconscious level? There is a way you can test subconscious beliefs called muscle testing or applied kinesiology. I'm going to briefly describe the method my clients have found to be the easiest and most reliable. First you stand up with your feet shoulder distance apart and face north. Then you say a statement or belief out loud. If the answer is "yes," your body will tilt forward and if the answer is "no," your body will tilt backward. You can start by saying, "My name is _____." Actually say your name and see what happens. Then say someone else's name and see what happens. If you tilt forward when you say your name, and backward when say someone else's name, you are ready to test a belief. Say something like, "All marriages end in divorce," or "My marriage will end in divorce." If you get "yes" to one or both of those beliefs, don't freak out. It is not a prediction of the future. It only tests whether or not you have that subconscious belief, and subconscious beliefs can be changed. There are many ways to muscle test. If you want to know more, there are many instructional videos on YouTube.

Are you ready to find out how to change subconscious beliefs? I will explain more in the next chapter.

Chapter 9:

Healing on a Deeper Level

*"Too many of us are not living our dreams
because we are living our fears."*
– Les Brown

Tammy's life and marriage was looking up because she started focusing on the positive aspects of her husband and her marriage. She had a daily meditation practice, was spending more time with her friend Elizabeth, and was taking better care of her body by exercising. She was feeling much more optimistic about Chad and staying in her marriage. But Tammy still felt fear when she thought about staying with Chad forever, and she felt fear when she thought about leaving him. She just couldn't make sense of where these feelings were coming from.

sense of some of them based on your past experiences, and some of these beliefs can come from your ancestors, your past lives, or the collective consciousness. Remember my client Susie who had the beliefs that "All men are abusive," and "I deserve to be abused?" She had those beliefs on a genetic level. That means she had the belief deeply imbedded in her subconscious mind, yet nothing had ever happened in this life that would have created those beliefs.

A term that therapists use very often with clients is "trigger." If your sister called you fat when you were a child and it upset you, someone calling you fat today could trigger that feeling from when you were a child. That is why you sometimes have what you might consider an overreaction to certain things. You are not aware of it, but it is triggering something deeper. This is also true if you have genetic or past-life trauma.

Many psychotherapists believe that gaining insight into what is being triggered from childhood can make the trigger lose its power or even disappear. For example, let's say you find out that the reason you get so angry when your partner disagrees with you is because it is triggering the way you felt when your father yelled at you when you were a child. Maybe your dad always had to be right and never let you have an opinion.

So, a psychotherapist might say that you can see your partner is not your dad, understand what is getting triggered when your partner disagrees with you, and decide not to let it upset you anymore. This could help for sure, but I find that it is too much work because you have to use your conscious mind to do it, when 95 percent of what is being triggered is actually subconscious. Also, I have found that just because you can sometimes find the trigger in this life, the likelihood that you don't also have something being triggered from a past life or on a genetic level is very slim.

Why Traditional Therapy Is So Hard

As I mentioned in Chapter 2, I was trained in a few different evidence-based interventions early in my career. One of these was Cognitive Behavioral Therapy, where you become aware of the thoughts that are making you unhappy and you change them to better-feeling thoughts. I've been talking about this concept throughout the book because it does change the way you feel, and it helps you create anything you want because of the Law of Attraction. Changing your thoughts, which changes the way you feel, can absolutely change your life. But I have found that for myself and some of my clients, it is hard to do. One explanation for why it can be hard is because you have to do it with your conscious mind. Did I mention that you are only functioning 5 percent out of your conscious mind? The other 95 percent is completely working against you, and guess which one normally wins?

When I was trained in all of those interventions, I was working for a PhD psychologist on a few different research studies. We recorded all of the sessions and watched them in supervision, and there was absolutely no way to deviate from the manual. I value that time because I learned so much about being a therapist, but I very much felt like I was in a box. I had a yearning to help people on a deeper level.

Traditional Therapy with a Kick

After the research studies ended, I had a job where I had the freedom to adopt a more eclectic view of therapy. I had been studying the Law of Attraction and realized how much it was in alignment with Cognitive Behavioral Therapy (CBT), so I didn't want to throw out the intervention completely. I started teaching clients EFT or tapping in conjunction with the CBT. So, we would focus on a thought that was upsetting, tap on it, and the emotion behind the thought would completely disappear. This made changing the thoughts easy for most of my clients. Try tapping out something that irritates you about your husband or wife and see if it makes it easier to see the situation differently.

Energy Healing Quickly Changes Subconscious Beliefs

At the same time that I was helping my clients change their thoughts with the help of tapping, I was exploring other types of energy healing techniques to use on myself. I started listening to teleconferences on how to make the Law of Attraction work more easily, and I bought several packages in order to explore different techniques.

When my husband and I got married, he moved into my house with his dog. I already had 2 dogs and I am a dog person, so I welcomed another dog. However, over time I noticed that his dog triggered anger in me. I tried to make sense of it by saying she had some annoying habits, but the anger I felt seemed to be triggering something I was not aware of from this lifetime. In one of the programs I purchased there was a trauma clearing. Since I didn't know what this was triggering for me, I decided to muscle test, "I have past life trauma that is being triggered by my husband's dog." I got a "yes," so I decided to experiment and go through the trauma clearing even though I didn't know what the trauma was at the time. To my amazement and surprise, my anger toward the dog completely vanished!

The trauma clearing worked so well it made me want to learn more. It seems like a small thing, and honestly I'm embarrassed to admit I felt that way about a sweet little dog, but it was a big thing for me given the fact that she was living in my house. I was also extremely intrigued that I didn't even have to know the specific trauma for it to *completely* disappear. It's literally like deleting it from a hard drive.

I flew out to Colorado to learn the technique myself, with the complete intention of only using it for self-healing. Honestly, I didn't really think I would be able to learn it, and it just seemed too good to be true. But I did learn how to clear beliefs, traumas, and fears. I felt like I had acquired a magic wand. Not using the magic wand proved to be difficult, actually impossible, when I returned to my clients.

I don't know if you read this in my bio or somewhere else, but I live in Arkansas. Arkansas is a very conservative state that is in the Bible Belt. A therapist using energy techniques intertwined with regular therapy didn't go over very well in the agency where I was working. They literally told me I was not allowed to do it. But, as I mentioned in chapter 2, my clients were loving it, and it was changing people's lives dramatically *and* fast. It was apparent that the next logical step for me was to go into private practice.

I have been amazed and surprised at how many people have been interested and open to exploring and experiencing these alternative methods. It is my passion to help people heal at a much deeper level than they ever imagined possible. I have explored several different healing techniques, which I continue to use in my practice. I have also developed my own healing technique, and I am excited to share with you.

The Process

Let's say you have the belief that you are not worthy or deserving of having a healthy marriage (On a side note: You would muscle test, "I am worthy and deserving of having a healthy marriage" because your subconscious mind does not understand negatives. If you get a "no" to that statement, then you believe you are not worthy or deserving of a healthy marriage). Using my technique, I would go in and delete that belief, all trauma associated with it, all of the fear, and any other negative feeling. I would do this through your entire life, your past lives, your genetics, the collective consciousness, and through your future and concurrent lives. Then I would release any oaths, vows, contracts, promises, obligations, commitments, debts, or liabilities related to it (I will explain this one in a minute). I would put you in the energy of forgiveness, forgiving anyone who hurt you related to any of this and anyone who you blamed for it, including yourself. I release any guilt, shame, anger, hatred, resentment, and any other feeling that comes up. Then I download the opposite belief into your subconscious, just like you would download something onto the hard drive of your computer (I know … sounds too good to be true, but it works!) I then ask you to get into the energy of knowing that you can be, do, or have *anything* you want, and I have you visualize life the way you want it.

I know the description of everything I clear is a lot, but that is why it will completely change your life. You don't have to remember any of it or even understand it for it to work, you just have to give the practitioner your permission to do the healing.

Let me explain the part about oaths, vows, contracts, promises, obligations, commitments, debts, and liabilities. I had a client named Judy who had been in an abusive marriage. She had dated a few men since her divorce, but couldn't seem to find anyone who she connected with enough to get married again. When we started digging, we discovered that she made a vow to never get married again. Our thoughts and words are very powerful. We say things like this all the time, but what we don't realize is that our sub-conscious mind is listening and recording everything. If you say you vow to never let that happen to you again, your subconscious could put a vow in place in order to protect you. Judy's vow was sabotaging her chances of meeting a healthy man who she would consider marrying. Just think about how many oaths, vows, contracts, promises, obligations, commitments, debts, and liabilities you have from past lives that you are unaware of.

Forgiveness Is for You

I also feel compelled to talk a little bit about for-giveness. I had a client named Kim whose father left her mother when she was 10 years old for another woman, and she had little to no contact with him after he left. Of course, Kim had a lot of work to do regarding abandonment, and beliefs about men and marriage, but she was also holding onto intense anger.

I asked Kim if she was ready to forgive her father for abandoning the family, and the answer was a big "*No*."

But what Kim needed to know, and what I want you to understand, is that holding onto anger and not forgiving someone is only hurting you. Do you think Kim's father was hurt by the fact that she didn't forgive him? He hadn't talked to Kim in years. Who do you think it was actually hurting? Yes, it was Kim. Holding onto anger and resentment can literally make a person physically ill, but it most definitely means that it can get triggered in all sorts of situations. So, do yourself a favor and decide to forgive people who have upset you. By the way, forgiving yourself for past mistakes is even more important. It's time to leave the past in the past, live in the present, and be eager to see what the future holds for you.

Forgiving is really just releasing resistance to who you really are. Let go and see how freeing it can be.

Chapter 10:

Obstacles

*"Nothing is impossible; the word itself says,
'I'm possible'!"*
– Audrey Hepburn

You Can Overcome Your Barriers

When I was leading The Incredible Years parent training groups, I had a client named Linda who often voiced a million reasons why she couldn't do the things I was asking her to do. She legitimately had a lot going on in her life. She was a single mom with three kids, and she had two jobs. Her main barrier was a lack of time and energy. When she brought up these obstacles, even though I knew following the curriculum would change her life, I just validated her feelings. I knew trying to convince her to follow the program was a waste of time. But Linda had committed to the 12-week program, so she begrudgingly did the work despite her time limitations.

Linda became one of my biggest success stories because she quickly realized that putting in the time on the front end paid off big time for her after only a few weeks. She started paying positive attention to her children instead of negative, and she noticed that her life had actually gotten much easier. Her kids started minding her more, started getting along with each other much better, and they were generally a lot more pleasant to be around. Not to mention, the older ones started helping around the house, which actually ended up saving her time.

If you are like Linda, you may feel like you don't have the time or energy to work on your marriage. It may just seem like it is too big of a bite to chew all by yourself. If you feel that way, you are like almost all of the people that I have helped save their marriages.

What do you think would have happened if Linda had waited for her kids to change before she could feel happy? When she realized that she could change her kids' behavior just by praising them and being more positive, she said she felt like she actually had *more* control.

Back when I was seeing Linda, I didn't know anything about the Law of Attraction. I just knew that paying positive attention to behavior would increase that behavior in children. But do you see the connection? When you pay attention to things you appreciate, you start feeling happy, and the universe brings more positive things into your life. There is something more going on here than positive reinforcement, though that is also a factor.

Release Resistance to Having a Happy Marriage

Let me get back to Linda's statement that she actually felt like she had more control. Control is something that I work on with my clients all the time. How do you feel about that word? You definitely don't want to lose control or be out of control, but how much do you try to control your partner or the way your marriage is going? The thing I want you to understand is that trying to control yourself, another person, or anything is not a good energy for you. Think about the analogy used by Abraham-Hicks of holding a cork underwater. If you are trying to control something, you are holding the cork underwater. If you stop trying to control things and just relax and think positively, you will feel happier and things will start to work out for you.

One of my favorite quotes by Henry Ford is, "Whether you believe you can or whether you believe you can't, you're right." How does this pertain to your marriage?

People are notoriously resistant to change. I think the main reason is because of the programming that is locked into place at such an early age. If you decide to change, you have to go against all of the subconscious programming that is deeply ingrained into you.

Tell a Different Story

I had a client named Stacy who was one of the most difficult clients I've ever worked with in my career. Stacy came to me after two failed marriages, and she was completely bitter not only about men, but about all people. She had deeply ingrained beliefs that people are liars, cheaters, and will manipulate anyone to get ahead. When we dug into those beliefs and released them, Stacy did not get better at first. I believe one of the reasons is because she was holding so strongly onto the belief that she is just a negative person, and nothing would ever change that fact. She could go on and on about how both of her parents and her sister are so negative. "That is just the way we are," she would often say.

What I want you to understand is that you are only the "way you are" because of all of your programming. You don't have to accept something like being a negative person. I worked with Stacy for several months, and she did eventually get better. She finally realized that her negative thinking was creating a life that she did not want, and that she could create a happy life by releasing resistance rather than pushing against everything she did not want. She ended up meeting a nice man, and she sent her sister to see me.

Change the Questions You Ask Yourself

I think another thing that keeps people stuck is the questions they ask themselves on a daily basis. Do you often find yourself asking questions like, "Why is marriage so hard? Why do I feel so angry? Why can't things just be like they were when we first got married?" When you ask yourself "why" questions, it is literally like you are giving your subconscious mind an assignment. Your subconscious mind gets to work to find out why these things are happening, which actually makes these things happen more.

What if instead you asked yourself questions like, "How can I improve my marriage?" or "How can I get that spark back and have the family I've always dreamed of?" Do you notice a difference in how you feel when you read those questions? If you ask yourself "how" questions, you are telling your subconscious mind there is a solution, and it goes to work to help you find it.

At this point as you read this book, I want you to think about the barriers you face in improving your marriage. What are the things you keep telling yourself that keep you feeling stuck and unhappy?

Following Through with Change

I have to wonder why people typically don't follow through with things to help themselves feel better. Resistance to change maybe? I bet most people would say it is a lack of time and energy, like my client Linda. But my best guess is that the real issue comes from some subconscious fear. It could be fear of a lot of things, like fear of the unknown, fear of failure, or even fear of success.

Some people need another person to hold them accountable for making changes. Let's look at Linda as an example again. She signed up for the class, and I would have known if she either didn't show up or didn't do the assignments. I didn't pressure her at all, but she did the work anyway and it paid off for her big time.

How much do you want to save your marriage? I wouldn't be surprised if you are having similar thoughts to Linda's, like you don't have the time or the energy to do the things I am recommending. The reason I'm guessing that is because it is completely normal. Sadly, it is human nature. Maybe it's a collective consciousness idea we're all plugged into. But I know you can see that if a single mom with three kids and two jobs can do it, so can you. Plus, changing your mindset about your partner doesn't actually take *any* time.

The people I have helped save their marriages had a few things in common. First of all, they could recall a time when they had an intense spark with their partner. At one time, they had common interests and a mutual respect for one another. But the main thing they had was an intense desire to stay in the marriage despite the problems they were having. If you have this desire too, I believe that you can overcome any obstacle. But remember, you have to take action. Marriage has to be nurtured. Are you ready to do what it takes to re-energize your passion?

Chapter 11:

Conclusion

*"Whatever you vividly imagine, ardently
desire, sincerely believe, and enthusiastically
act upon... must inevitably come to pass!"*
– Paul J. Meyer

You Can Be a Success Story Too

After Tammy realized how much her thoughts were affecting how she felt about her marriage, she was able to remind herself of the things she saw in Chad when they first started dating. She started realizing that she didn't have to spend more time with Chad in order to feel more connected. She just had to put energy out toward him when they were together. Everything about their relationship improved, and they developed a love that was deeper than they had at the beginning. They started talking about their hopes and dreams, and fantasized about all the things they could do together in the future.

With my help, Tammy was able to become aware of the subconscious beliefs and fears she was holding onto that were sabotaging her marriage. She started feeling much more confident in herself, which made her feel happier in every area of her life. Appreciating the positive aspects of her life became second nature to Tammy, and she eventually began seeing evidence that she is the deliberate creator of her life. She no longer felt like life was just happening to her.

Tammy and Chad stayed together and had the family they had always dreamed of. As problems came up, Tammy would get back to the basics and turn things around before ever feeling trapped and terrified as she had before. She had sessions with me to work on her beliefs and fears about having kids, and she was not always the perfect mother or wife, but she no longer beat herself up when she made a mistake. She would just take things as they came and would intentionally get back on track.

Tammy's new positive outlook rubbed off on Chad even though he didn't do anything consciously to work on their marriage. Plus, Tammy got the best version of Chad by appreciating his positive qualities and feeling happy in their relationship again. If you asked Tammy today, I know she would say she successfully got the passion back in her marriage and in her life.

What If I Married the Wrong Person?

Something I have not mentioned is what to do if the story of my first marriage resonates with you, and you think you should get a divorce too. I once heard a woman say, when you get a divorce and marry someone else, you trade in one set of problems for another. The best thing you can do right now is work on the marriage you are in. If it doesn't result in you becoming happy in your marriage, the effort will not be wasted.

Remember that one of the subconscious beliefs I had from childhood was "Even happy marriages end in divorce." What do you think would have happened if I had changed that belief while I was still in my first marriage? Honestly, I don't know if there was any way I could have saved that marriage, but I do know that the same fears would not have been triggered in my second marriage if I had already worked on them.

The exception to my advice about working on the marriage you are in is if you are in an abusive relationship. If that is the case, please seek the help of a professional who can help you safely leave your marriage. If you need assistance in finding a professional, please contact me so I can help.

Things to Remember

I hope this book has given you insight into the reasons why you are having problems in your marriage. Remember, you are the creator of your own reality, therefore you can be, do, or have anything you want, *including* a happy marriage. The Law of Attraction is always working whether you are aware of it or not.

Make a conscious effort to care about how you feel. Do more things you enjoy, with your partner, alone, and with friends. Spending time doing activities that fill you up is a good way to ensure you feel better about your life. Pamper yourself, and remember it is not selfish.

Become aware of your thoughts as much as you can. Notice how much better you feel when you think more positive thoughts, such as appreciating the things you love about your life and your partner. When you are feeling angry or irritable, try to get into an energy of appreciation. Sometimes it requires taking a nap or distracting yourself to pull you out of a bad mood, so give yourself what you need, and know that every day is a new opportunity to create the relationship you desire.

Start a daily practice of self-care. Getting into a routine of meditating, doing Qigong, or tapping could completely change your life and your relationship. Exercise is also a way to increase endorphins. Some people say that exercise can have the same effect as taking an anti-depressant. Remember to pick something and start doing it regularly rather than waiting until you have a crisis in your life.

Take the Love Languages quiz online and have your partner take it too. If you are both mindful of the way you give and receive love, it could completely turn your marriage around.

Try to be assertive when you can and notice when you are using a different communication style. Noticing things that could be improved in your marriage is the first step.

Remember that your subconscious mind is running the show. Know that changing some deeply imbedded subconscious beliefs makes everything else I have recommended easier.

Where to Go from Here

> *"If you keep doing what you've always done,*
> *you'll keep getting what you've always got."*
> – W.L. Bateman

I hope this book has inspired you to see your marriage and your life in a different light. But what I want for you is more than shifting the way you see things. I want you to have an action plan to completely change your marriage.

If you put this book on the shelf and hope that you remember all the ways to change your marriage, you will likely feel better for a while, but lasting change takes more effort. You need support. You need people who you can talk to about these new ideas. If your partner is willing to read and discuss this book with you, get them involved. If not, find a friend to share these ideas with, and start talking about all the positive things in your life. You have to get out of the mindset and habit of focusing on the negative things about your relationship because it makes you attract more negative things into your life.

If you want to find out more about changing your subconscious beliefs, know that I am here to help. It is my dream to make more people aware that deeper healing is possible, and to help people find healing that resonates with them. You can find me at www. lovetheoneyourewith.com

There is absolutely no reason to suffer through an unhappy marriage. Now you have all the information you need to get that spark back in your marriage and in your life, so go get started!

Acknowledgments

From a very young age I thought I would write a book, though I had no idea what it would be about. Over the last couple of years, the information in this book has been rolling around in my head. I knew what I wanted to say, but I had no idea how to put it together. It took the love and support of many people to help me get it written.

With love and gratitude, I want to acknowledge:

Angela Lauria, thank you for putting together a program that made writing a book so manageable for a busy person like me. Ora North and Anna Paradox, thank you for being so patient and supportive, and at the same time, keeping me on track. Cheyenne Giesecke, thank you for just being so awesome.

The Morgan James Publishing team: Special thanks to David Hancock, CEO & Founder for believing in me and my message. To my Author Relations Manager, Bonnie Rauch, thanks for making the process seamless and easy. Many more thanks to everyone else, but especially Jim Howard, Bethany Marshall, and Nickcole Watkins.

All of my clients. I have learned so much from each and every one of you. Without you, this book would not have been possible.

My entire family. Thank you for always being supportive of my path in life.

All of the friends, teachers, therapists, and healers who have been there for me throughout the years. There are too many to mention specifically, so below I am naming a few who have been there through the process of me writing this book.

Shannon Dillon who helped me realize it was time to write a book, for helping me find The Author Incubator, and for healing my fears throughout the process.

Jenn Daughty, who helped me clear all of the blocks that came up while writing this book. I can't imagine how I would have done it without you.

Debby Zarzour, for always seeing the best in me and lifting me up when I was feeling down. Thank you for pushing me to learn new things and to see things from a new perspective.

Betsy Johnson, who has been there for me every step along the way on my journey. Thank you for always listening and supporting my growth through this process.

My paddle boarding buddies, Paula Mallory, Denise Barton, and Marianna O'dea, for listening to me talk about my book on every excursion.

Jen Witt, who was held captive in Arkansas for the summer after having a terrible mountain biking accident. Thanks for listening to me talk about my book for countless hours. You will be one of my paddle boarding buddies next year!

Lloyd Ellis, who was also held captive after Jen's accident. Thank you for being so loving and supportive while I wrote this book.

Tiffany Livingston, who has shared in my joy and helped me with all of my "technical" difficulties. Your book is next!

Thank You

Thanks so much for reading. I've been really excited to share this information with people who want to save their marriage. The fact that you have made it this far tells me you are one of those people.

To support you in working on your marriage, I have created an assessment to help you figure out where you are in your relationship and where you want to be. I have also created a video class to help you get started.

To receive these free gifts, just visit my website: LoveTheOneYoureWith.com

I'll see you there!

Lee

About the Author

Lee Ellis is a licensed mental health professional in the state of Arkansas. Having gone through a divorce by the age of 30, Lee felt compelled to figure out what went wrong in her marriage and how to make a marriage work. She set out to discover the answers for herself, and realized she could use the techniques that worked so well for her on her clients. Since then, she has helped numerous people become happy in their relationships and in their lives.

Lee lives in Little Rock, Arkansas with her husband and daughter where she has a thriving private practice. She spends much of her spare time kayaking, paddle boarding, and hiking with her family and friends. She also enjoys meditation, yoga, and listening to Abraham-Hicks or other spiritual teachers.

Lee is passionate about helping other people find the happiness that she has found in her personal and professional life. She sees a growing need to get her message out there and she is ready to share it with you.